The Legend of JESSIE HICKMAN

MARK GREENWOOD

FRANÉ LESSAC

NATIONAL LIBRARY OF AUSTRALIA PUBLISHING

Jessie grew up in a travelling bush circus with clowns and acrobats, buckjump horses and a hee-haw donkey. She was feisty and fearless, and taught herself daring skills.

If you believe in legends, Jessie could walk the tightrope before she was eight years old.

Rain or shine, circus wagons were always on the move, bouncing along bumpy bush tracks. In frontier towns, the troupe would hoist the big top and prepare the sawdust floor while Jessie practiced somersaults and pirouettes.

The circus made people happy. Children howled with laughter at the cartwheeling clowns. They cheered for Cleo the Snake Charmer, draped in pythons and cuddling a crocodile. At the age of ten, Jessie was cracking stockwhips.

By the time she was eleven, Jessie was
a sharpshooter with a steady hand,
bursting balloons floating above the crowd.

‘The Amazing Miss Jessie’ was soon the star of the show. In a sequined costume, with a hint of fire in the frizz of her hair, she performed handstands on a bare-backed pony.

If you believe in legends, Jessie was only fourteen when she was declared 'Australian Champion Rough Rider'.

But the drums of the Great War were beating. Ticket sales dwindled. In tough times, the circus struggled to draw happy crowds. Jessie leaned on the shoulder of her favourite horse, Houdini. 'We're on our own now,' she said.

Years rolled by. With no place to call home, Jessie drifted into the craggy mountains. There she put her circus skills to use. She tucked her knotty hair under a hat and cracked her stockwhip. Under a sky full of stars, Jessie drove bellowing herds of stolen cattle along treacherous trails.

At the saleyards, Jessie wore a velvet frock trimmed with lace.
Locals steered clear of the gun-toting lady in snakeskin boots.
It was rumoured she could shoot backwards, sideways, even blindfolded.

If you believe in legends, the lady bushranger always galloped away with a fistful of cash.

Jessie and Houdini zigzagged through the Blue Mountains, along narrow, winding ravines. With grass for a pillow and a commanding view of the valley, she camped in a cave where no one could find her.

The gullies and ridges soon echoed with the sound of police patrols. Wanted posters offered a reward for the capture of 'The Lady Bushranger'. But Jessie led the troopers on a merry dance. To give 'em the slip, she once rode Houdini over a cliff, into a raging river. 'Catch me if you can!' she hollered.

609
SECOND

Police set traps, but Jessie vanished like a ghost into the misty mountains. 'She's a wild one,' the troopers barked. 'Hunt her down.' If you believe in legends, Jessie once escaped custody by leaping from a moving train.

Troopers tracked the lady bushranger across a deep gorge, into a canyon walled by granite boulders. 'Give yourself up!' they shouted. Jessie boxed like a kangaroo and kicked like a mule until she was handcuffed.

In court, a judge banged his gavel and sentenced Jessie to a year in prison. She stared at dust dancing in the sunbeams and dreamed of better days to come.

After her release, Jessie built a tumbledown hut at Emu Creek. Woodsmoke curled up from the chimney. A rickety lean-to kept Houdini warm.

Jessie was kind to all the bush critters and well-known for sharing a pot of bubbling stew with hungry families in the area. 'She's a good outlaw,' her neighbours agreed.

Often, when a cow went missing, Jessie's friends hid the evidence from the troopers who came to arrest her. The judge was not amused. Without proof, he had no choice but to wave a warning with his crooked finger and pronounce the lady bushranger, 'Not Guilty'.

Jessie enjoyed the stillness that settled around her humble home. Occasionally she took her beloved horse for a gallop through the ghost gums. With a hint of fire in the frizz of her hair, she performed handstands on Houdini's back. If you believe in legends, the lady was the last bushranger.

ELIZABETH JESSIE HICKMAN (1890–1936)

Also known as:

- Elizabeth Jessie Hunt
- Jessie McIntyre
- Jessie Bell
- Jessie Payne
- Jessie Glen Thomas
- Mrs Bell
- Mrs Hudson
- Mrs Murray
- Mrs Martini
- 'Lizzie'

TIMELINE

1890 Elizabeth 'Jessie' Hunt is born at Burraga, New South Wales.

1898 Joins a travelling bush circus.

1902 Learns to crack stockwhips, shoot a rifle and the art of trick riding.

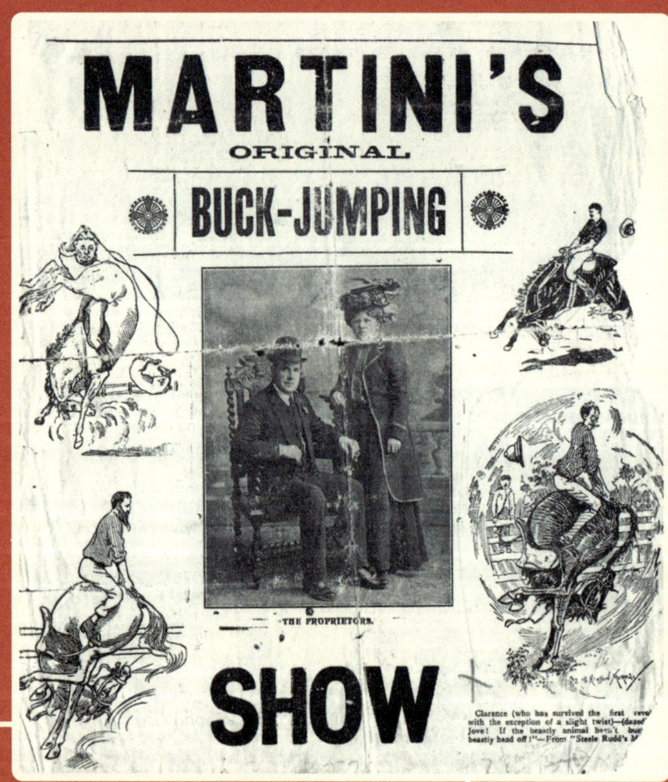

1904 'The Amazing Miss Jessie' is the star of Martini's Buck-Jumping Show.

1906 Named 'Australian Women's Rough Riding Champion'.

1910 Martini's Buck-Jumping Show closes.

TRAVELLING CIRCUS

The first recorded performance of tightrope walking was given in Sydney in 1833. Later, circuses presented acrobats, animals, clowns and feats of horsemanship. The travelling bush circus provided remote country towns with entertainment for the whole family.

BUSHRANGERS

To survive in tough times, a bushranger had to be cunning and quick-witted, not to mention highly skilled at riding horses and shooting a rifle. Besides Jessie Hickman, other well-known lady bushrangers include Indigenous outlaws Mary Cockerill and Mary Ann Bugg.

BUCKJUMPING

The origins of Australian rodeo can be traced back to outback stations boasting a horse that 'couldn't be ridden'. The best rough riders went on to make a living in buckjump shows and travelling circuses. Today, the rodeo is a sporting highlight in many rural and regional communities.

No. 13150 Name Jessie McIntyre alias Bell

Date when Portrait was taken 15-8-1913. Payne

Native place Bathurst

Year of birth 6-9-91

Arrived in Colony B.S

Trade or occupation previous to conviction Dom. duties

Religion C of E

Education, degree of R and W

Height, without shoes 5 ft 6 inches

Weight 153

Colour of hair Dark brown

Colour of eyes Brown

Marks or special features nil

(No. of previous Portrait)

CONVICTIONS.

Where and When.	Offence.	Sentence.
Parramatta Q.S. 15.8.13	Horsestealing	12 months L.L.

Vide Police Gazette, 1926, pages 629 and 694, and 1927, page 54.

ELIZABETH HICKMAN, alias JESSIE McINTYRE, alias MRS. BELL, alias MRS. HUDSON, alias G. MURRAY, charged on warrant with stealing six head of cattle, the property of James Frederick Mills, has been arrested by Sergeant 2nd Class Buckley and Constable Smith, Rylstone and Wollar Police. Further charged with stealing two cows, the property of Roy Halpin and Allan Doyle Willis respectively. Committed for trial on the first two charges at Mudgee Sessions, and discharged on the other.

1913 Charged with stealing cattle and sentenced to 12 months in Long Bay Reformatory.

1916 Charged with theft and sentenced to one year and nine months in gaol.

1918 Charged with cattle stealing but is acquitted.

1920 Marries Benjamin Hickman but they separate after she refuses to leave the bush.

1926 Warrant issued against her for stealing five cows and a calf.

1928 Arrested at Emu Creek and charged with stealing. Acquitted on lack of evidence.

1936 Jessie dies and is buried in an unmarked grave at Sandgate Cemetery, Newcastle.

GLOSSARY

Big top the main tent in a circus
Buckjumping an event in which a rider attempts to stay in the saddle of a bucking horse
Bushranger an outlaw living in the bush
Cattle duffing in Australia, the act of stealing cattle
Evidence facts that prove or disprove something
Frontier town a remote country town bordering bushland or the outback
Gavel a small hammer used by a judge to call for attention or order
Great War The First World War (1914–1918)
Judge a public officer appointed to decide cases in a court of law
Jury a group of people sworn to deliver a verdict in court
Outlaw a person who has broken the law and remains a fugitive
Pirouette spinning on one foot with the raised foot touching the knee of the supporting leg
Rough rider someone who rides unbroken or untrained horses
Sharpshooter a person skilled in shooting
Snake charmer an entertainer who uses snakes in a performance
Stockwhip a whip usually used for driving cattle
Tightrope a rope or wire stretched tightly above the ground on which acrobats balance
Travelling bush circus a travelling troupe of entertainers such as acrobats, clowns and trapeze artists
Trooper a mounted police officer
Troupe a group of dancers, actors or entertainers who perform at different venues

For Araminta and Addison

With special thanks to Lauren Smith, Amelia Hartney, Madeleine Warburton, Julie Hally, Marcia Wernick, National Library of Australia reference librarians Lisa Sammut and Matthew Stuckings, Claire Bartley from the Stockman's Hall of Fame and Jane Gibian from the State Library of New South Wales.

Published by National Library of Australia Publishing
Canberra ACT 2600

ISBN: 9781922507853

The National Library of Australia acknowledges Australia's First Nations Peoples—the First Australians—as the Traditional Owners and Custodians of this land and gives respect to the Elders—past and present—and through them to all Australian Aboriginal and Torres Strait Islander people.

First Nations Peoples are advised this book contains names of deceased people.

Publisher: Lauren Smith
Managing editor: Amelia Hartney
Designer: Julie Hally
Image coordinator: Madeleine Warburton
Printed in China by R.R. Donnelley on FSC®-certified paper.

Image credits: 'Miss Kemp wearing a lace top and long pants tucked into knee-high boots', *The Queenslander* (Brisbane), 3 February 1906, SLQ; *Gaol Inmates/Prisoners Photos Index 1870–1930*, 1913, MHNSW, NRS2138; *New South Wales Police Gazette and Weekly Record of Crime* (Sydney), 16 May 1928, p.322, nla.news-page28005468; *Martini's Buck-jumping Show handbill*, c.1910, in *Thorpe McConville's Wild Australia* by Ray McConville (Myrtleford: Vic, 1997), nla.cat-vn170554.

Find out more about NLA Publishing at library.gov.au/discover/nla-publishing.
A catalogue record for this book is available from the National Library of Australia.